An ~~Illustrated~~ ~~Guide~~ to

Mythical Creatures

A brief introduction to the varied life-forms of hearsay found in the myths, legends and folklore of cultures around the world, with illustrations by David West and text by Anita Ganeri.

An Illustrated Guide to Mythical Creatures
was produced by

David West ☂ Children's Books
7 Princeton Court
55 Felsham Road
London SW15 1AZ

Designed and illustrated by David West
Written by Anita Ganeri and David West

First published in the UK in MMIX *by* Book House,
an imprint of The Salariya Book Company Ltd.,
25, Marlborough Place, Brighton BN1 1UB

SALARIYA

Please visit the Salariya Book Company at:
www.book-house.co.uk

11 10 09 08 07
10 9 8 7 6 5 4 3 2 1

ISBN: 978 1 9067 1442 0 (hardback)
ISBN: 978 1 9067 1441 3 (paperback)

A CIP catalogue record for this book is available from the British Library.

Photo Credits:
12tr, Hector Joseph Lumang; 12bl, Lynn Watson; 43ml, Sander Kamp; 43br, David Evans

Printed and bound in China.

Contents

Introduction

Herein lies a magical world of strange creatures and fabulous beasts, where the Cockatrice's glance can turn a person to stone, and the trumpet of the Manticore lures unsuspecting travellers to their doom. Here be knights riding Hippogriffs, heroes battling dragons, Scorpion men guarding the tombs of the dead, and giants fighting gods.

Dare to turn the pages of this book to discover a world of myth and legend brought to life in beautiful colour illustrations.

A knight battles a dragon to rescue a maiden.

Dragons, Serpents & Worms

Y Ddraig Gosh, the Welsh red dragon

Here be dragons...Dragons appear in almost every mythology around the world, as immense, lizard-like beasts covered in scales. They hatch from eggs after thousands of years, and are sometimes said to spit poison or breathe fire.

Dragons East and West

As with most creatures of myth, dragons are understood and depicted in different ways by different cultures. Eastern dragons are very powerful but usually benevolent. They are revered for their great wisdom, and are often worshipped as mythical rulers of nature and the weather, particularly of water and rain. Unlike Western dragons, these dragons do not have wings because it is believed that they fly by magic.

In the mythologies of the West, most dragons are dangerous. Some live in caves where they fiercely guard hoards of gold and treasure. Others terrorise towns and villages, demanding human sacrifices to eat. Unlike Eastern dragons, there are numerous legends of these terrible beasts being hunted down and killed. Dragon slayers are famous and heroic characters in Western folklore. In Greek mythology, Prince Cadmus is sent in search of his missing sister, Europa. He fails to find her but decides to found a city on a spot guarded by a serpent-like dragon, which he kills. In medieval times, there were many famous dragon slayers like Siegfried, hero of the German Niebelungenlied. He kills the dragon, Fafnir, and drinks its blood. This makes him invulnerable, apart from one small spot on his shoulder.

In Eastern mythology, the Azure Dragon is one of the four symbols of the constellation. It represents the East, spring and the element of wood.

One of the most famous dragon slayers of Christian folklore is St George, shown in the 15th-century Russian icon above. Legend says that he killed a dragon which was about to devour the king's daughter.

Eastern dragons, like the one in this Japanese dragon shrine, are often shown with a large pearl in their grasp, though some say that it is really the dragon's egg.

Wyverns and Lindworms

The legendary Wyvern differs from the European dragon. It has only two legs, large wings instead of front limbs, and sometimes with eagle's claws on the tips. It is unsure whether Wyverns breathe fire, like dragons, but they have deadly arrow-shaped barbs at the ends of their tails for killing their prey. In medieval Europe, Wyverns were associated with war, pestilence and plague. As heraldic emblems they usually depict strength and endurance. The closely-related Lindworms of Scandinavian and German mythology are often described as having the body of a serpent and a poisonous bite. These enormous and terrifying beasts eat cattle, and are believed to raid churchyards to devour the dead.

Since 1730, the Zilant, a Wyvern, has been the official emblem of Kazan, Russia.

Wyverns are said to be more aggressive than dragons and to prey on humans and livestock.

Worms

In northern European mythology, the word for dragon is 'worm' which means snake or serpent. In old English, it is 'wyrm'. Legends from the Middle Ages describe Worms as serpents with no wings or legs but with dragons' heads. The tale of the Lambton Worm tells how John Lambton catches a Worm while out fishing in the local river, and throws it down a nearby well. Over the years, the beast grows to a huge size and attacks the local livestock and villagers. Many knights die trying to slay the beast. Finally, John Lambton succeeds in killing the Worm.

Lambton fights the Worm by the river so that the water carries away the pieces of the beast before they can join up to form its body again.

Quetzalcoatl devouring a man from the Codex Telleriano-Remensis.

Feathered Serpent

Quetzalcoatl, the feathered serpent, was a god in Aztec mythology, religion and art. Often depicted as a snake with a headdress made from quetzal bird feathers, Quetzalcoatl was also the wind god, the patron god of priests and responsible for the creation of the world.

Many-headed Serpents

In Ancient Greek legend, the hero, Heracles, is set the task of killing the Hydra, a huge snake with numerous heads, and breath so poisonous it can kill human beings. On reaching Lake Lerna, Heracles fires burning arrows into the Hydra's lair to draw out the monstrous beast. But each time Heracles cuts off one of its heads, two more heads grow in its place. Heracles calls on his nephew, Ioalus, for help. After each head is cut off, Ioalus seals the stump with a burning branch until, at last, the Hydra is dead. In a later task, Heracles also kills the hundred-headed serpent, Ladon, which guards the Garden of Hesperides, in order to steal the apples of immortality.

The Garden of Hesperides, painted by Frederic Leighton.

Heracles battles with the Hydra, a many-headed serpent.

Giant Serpents

Many cultures have myths describing giant serpents that do battle with the gods. These conflicts often represent the struggle of good versus evil. Apep, a giant serpent from Ancient Egyptian myths embodies all that is evil. Representing darkness and chaos, he is the arch enemy of order and light. Every night, as the Sun god, Ra, sinks below the horizon, he does battle with Apep in the underworld but always returns victorious to the morning sky.

In Norse mythology, Jormungandr, the sea serpent, is so enormous that he can encircle Midgard (the world) and hold his own tail in his mouth. He is greatly feared by sailors. Jormungandr's arch enemy is Thor, the god of thunder. Once when Thor goes fishing with the giant, Hymir, Hymir warns him that they are in danger. Thor ignores the giant's warning and casts his line, baited with an ox's head, which Jormungandr snatches. After a great struggle, Thor pulls the serpent from the water, and is about to kill him when Hymir cuts the line and it escapes.

A painting of Thor fighting the Midgard serpent, by Henry Fuseli.

An Ancient Egyptian painting showing a god warding off the serpent, Apep.

Roger rides a Hippogriff to rescue Angelique.

Flying Creatures

Folk tales, myths, legends and heraldry are filled with examples of fantastical flying creatures and winged beasts.

None is more majestic that the fabulous Griffin, with the body of a lion, and the head and wings of an eagle.

An illustration of a Griffin by Sir John Tenniel for Lewis Carroll's Alice in Wonderland.

A Peryton

Part Bird...

Tales of Griffins reached Europe from ancient Scythia where these legendary beasts were said to line their nests with gold, killing anyone who dared steal it from them. In medieval times, it was believed that a Griffin's feathers and claws had magical powers. The feathers were thought to cure blindness. A cup made from a griffin claw could warn of the presence of poison by changing colour. Rarer still than the Griffin was the Hippogriff, the offspring of a Griffin and a horse.

Another mythical bird-like beast was the Peryton which had the forelegs, head, and antlers of a stag, and the wings, feathers and back legs of a bird.

In Persian mythology, the Simurgh is a bird with a dog's head and lion's claws. Its wings are so huge that they could block out the sun.

The Simurgh

One of the most famous flying creatures of all is Pegasus, the winged horse of ancient Greek mythology who carries the hero, Bellerophon, to kill the Chimera (see page 17). A similar winged horse, known as Buraq, appears in Islamic literature and art.

This 17th-century Mughal miniature shows Buraq as a winged horse, with the head of a woman.

Pegasus and Bellerophon

Other winged creatures

The Hsigo, or Hsaio, a monkey with wings, appears in Chinese folklore. Its presence is believed to warn of serious drought. Human-headed lions and bulls, called Shedu or Lamassu, come from Ancient Assyria. Sculptures of these creatures were placed as guardians at the entrances of cities and palaces.

Hsigos in flight

A sculpture of a Lamassu from Ancient Assyria

Harpies and Sirens

Bird-like creatures with human heads appear in mythology throughout the world. Among the most terrible are the Harpies of Ancient Greece. They torment humans by stealing their food and screeching so that their victims cannot eat or rest. Supposedly, the only thing they feared was the sound made by a brass instrument.
Sirens look similar to Harpies but they used their beautiful singing voice to lure sailors to their deaths on the rocks. In Russian mythology, they were known as Sirins.

Sirin (left) and Alkonost, birds of joy and sorrow, by Vicktor Vasnetsov (1896)

In this 1891 painting by John William Waterhouse, the Greek hero, Odysseus, tied to the mast, survives the Sirens' song. On the advice of an enchantress, he blocks the ears of his men with bees' wax so that they cannot hear their fateful music.

Giant Birds

The Roc was an enormous mythical bird so strong that it was believed to be able to carry off and eat elephants. The legend of the Roc reached the West through Marco Polo's account of his travels, and the story of Sinbad the Sailor. The legend may have been inspired by the elephant bird of Madagascar which became extinct in the 16th century.

The Vucub-Cacquix ('Seven Macaw'), the Mayan giant bird-demon, claimed to be the Sun and the Moon; the Chinese Peng could fly for six months without resting; and the Ziz from Jewish mythology had wings that could block out the sun.

In The 1001 Nights, *Sinbad the Sailor's ship is destroyed by a Roc.*

Fire and Thunder Birds

In Native North American legend, the Thunderbird is a mythical bird of immense power and strength. It is believed that the beating of its huge wings causes the sound of thunder and that lightning flashes from its eyes. Similarly, the South African Impundulu, or 'lightning bird', is a black and white bird, the size of a human, which summons thunder and lightning with its wings and claws.

Perhaps the most famous firebird is the fabulous Phoenix that features in many myths. There is only one Phoenix at a time, although it lives for hundreds of years. At the end of its life the bird and its nest burn to ashes, from which a new, young Phoenix arises.

In Russian mythology, the Firebird is a large bird with glowing feathers.

A Phoenix painted on the walls of a tower used for burnt offerings in Tian Hou Temple, Shenzhen, Guangdon, China.

Images of the Thunderbird are popular in Native North American art and often appear carved on totem poles.

Prince Ivan returns from his quest on a magic carpet with a caged Firebird, by Viktor Vasnetsov.

13

Messengers of the Gods

Hermes is the Greek god who acts as a messenger between the gods of Mount Olympus and human beings. He is given this task by Apollo, to keep him out of trouble. He is shown wearing winged sandals and a winged helmet to speed his flight between the worlds of the mortals and immortals. Hermes is also the protector of travellers and thieves. In Roman mythology, the equivalent deity is Mercury.

Hermes

Eros

Since ancient times, human-like creatures with wings have featured in the world's myths and legends. In Greek mythology, Eros is sometimes said to be the son of Ares, god of war, and Aphrodite, goddess of beauty. This mischievous god specialises in making people fall in love by piercing them with his golden arrows. He himself falls in love with a beautiful woman, called Psyche, when he grazes himself on one of his own arrows. In Roman mythology, he becomes Cupid, a young boy with his bow and arrows in hand.

Eros had two kinds of arrows. His golden arrows with dove feathers caused people to fall in love instantly. His lead arrows with owl feathers led to disinterest.

Garuda

In Hindu mythology, Garuda is usually shown with the body of a man but the wings and beak of an eagle. The king of the birds, he is often chosen to carry the great god, Vishnu. He is the enemy of snakes and Nagas (see page 24).

Garuda's story is told in the great Hindu sacred text, The Mahabharata, in which he is a symbol of speed and military strength. Huge birds, called Garudas, also appear in Buddhist mythology. They are said to create hurricane-force winds when they flap their gigantic wings.

Worshipping Garuda is believed to cleanse the body of poisons.

Angels

Angels are supernatural beings found in many religions. In Christianity, Islam and Judaism, they are heavenly beings, created by God, who are sent down to Earth to instruct people about God's wishes or to perform other tasks. Angels are often shown as human-like creatures with wings. In Islamic belief, angels are made by Allah (God) from light but can take on any form they choose, human or otherwise. They are neither male nor female, and are immortal.

In the 17th-century painting by Guido Reni, the archangel Michael is shown in military dress as he fights against Satan.

Tengus

Tengus are spirit-like creatures which appear in many different forms in Japanese folklore. They are usually shown with both bird-like and human characteristics, including a bright red face and extremely long nose. Tengus take their name from a fierce dog-like demon in Chinese mythology which brought war and caused thunder. In early Japanese stories, they were enemies of Buddhism, kidnapping monks and robbing temples. They later returned their victims, in a state of madness or near-death. In later tales, Tengus are divided into good and bad spirits. Some religious groups worshipped them as gods who protected sacred mountains and forests.

A 19th-century woodprint by Utagawa Kuniyoshi, showing an elephant catching a flying Tengu.

A Leyak

Flying Heads

In the mythology of Bali, Leyaks are hideous flying creatures that haunt graveyards and feed on dead bodies. By day, they appear as ordinary humans. At night, their gruesome heads and entrails break out of their bodies and fly.

One look from the Cockatrice can turn a person to stone.

Chimera

Chimera are creatures made of the parts of different animals. The name comes from the Chimera of Greek mythology, a fire-breathing beast with the head of a lion, the head of a goat on its back and the tail of a serpent.

The Chimera's father was Typhon, god of the wind, and its mother Echidna, a monster who was part-woman, part-snake. It is eventually killed by the hero, Bellerophon, riding Pegasus, the winged horse (see page 11).

Mixed up Creatures

Mythologies around the world have thrown up bizarre and outlandish Chimera. The Ahuizotl of Aztec myth is an extraordinary creature that is half-dog, half-monkey with a human hand at the end of its tail. Believed to live near water, it snatches and eats people who venture too close to the water's edge, or fishermen in their boats.

In Japanese mythology, a Nue is a beast with a monkey's head, a raccoon dog's body, a tiger's legs and a snake for a tail. It is said that a Nue can change itself into a black cloud and fly, bringing bad luck and illness.

One of the most feared Chimera is the Cockatrice. This dreaded creature resembles a large cockerel, with dragon's wings and a serpent's tail. Its magic powers include a deadly stare that can kill people or turn them to stone. It can only be killed if its stare is reflected back at it from a polished surface, or if it hears a cockerel crow. The weasel, the Cockatrice's arch enemy, is the only animal that can survive its gaze.

A stone plaque dating from around 1500 from a temple at Tepoztlan, south of Mexico City, which shows the Ahuizotl.

A woodprint from 1852 showing a Nue, disguised as a black cloud, descending on the royal palace.

A woodblock print of a a snake-like Chimera, the Basilisk, from 1642.

Ammit is composed of three animals which the Ancient Egyptians considered to be particularly dangerous.

More bizarre beasts

The most improbable Chimera of all is the Mermecolion, a creature that is half-lion, half-ant. It never feeds because each half craves what the other half cannot eat so it quickly starves to death. The Ammit of Ancient Egyptian myths is a mixture of three animals – the lion, crocodile and hippo. Believed to inhabit the underworld, Ammit devours the hearts of wrong-doers. The Sphinx of Ancient Egypt is usually shown with the body of a lion and a human head. Regarded as guardians, statues of sphinxes were placed outside temples and royal tombs. They also appear in Asian mythologies, where they are known as 'man-cats' or 'man-lions'.

Mermecolion

Egyptian Sphinxes are shown in one of these three forms:

Hierocosphinx - body of lion with head of hawk or falcon

Criosphinx - body of lion with head of ram

Androsphinx - body of lion with head of human being

Other bizarre Chimera, called Serpopards, appear in Ancient Egyptian carvings. They seem to be leopards with the heads and necks of snakes. With their necks intertwined, these creatures may have been considered a symbol for the unification of Egypt.

From India and Africa, stories have emerged of a Rompo, a Chimera that feeds on corpses. It has the head of a hare with human ears, and a metre-long body with a long tail. It has the front legs of a badger and the back legs of a bear. It visits graveyards at night to circle the graves before it starts digging…

Rompo

Two Serpopards with intertwining necks appear on the Narmer Palette which dates from the 31st century BC. Two men hold ropes, tied to the Serpopards' necks.

Heraldic Beasts

Chimera have appeared as heraldic symbols on many crests and shields. These beasts have specific meanings - lions represent strength and courage; horses are symbols of readiness for duty. Animals are combined to give greater significance. An Alphyn has a lion's head and body, with an eagle's claws and a long tongue. The Calygreyhound symbolises swiftness. It is said to have the body of a deer, the front legs of an eagle, the back legs and hooves of an ox, and the head of a wild cat. Another heraldic beast is the Enfield which has the head of a fox, a greyhound's chest, a lion's body, the back legs and tail of a wolf, and eagle's claws on its front legs.

Alphyn

Calygreyhound

Enfield

The legendary Ypotryll is a heraldic Chimera with a boar's head and tusks, a camel's humped body, the legs of a goat or ox, and a serpent's tail.

The Questing Beast

In Arthurian legend, the Questing Beast is a strange creature that many brave knights 'quest', or attempt to hunt. The beast is sometimes said to resemble a leopard, with a serpent's head and neck, a lion's tail and back legs, and a deer's hooves.

Some knights dedicated their lives to their search for the Questing Beast.

The Good

Most mythical creatures have been born out of human fears. A few, however, break this mould. The Unicorn of Western myth is one such legendary beast. Popularly, a Unicorn was seen as a beautiful white or grey horse-like creature with a single, spiral horn growing from its forehead. In fact it was a Chimera made up of a horse, with a goat's cloven hooves and a lion's tail. It was thought to be a magical beast with healing powers. Its horn detects poison in food and drink, and then purifies it. The horn was so valuable that the Unicorn was hunted to extinction. A maiden was used to enchant the Unicorn so that it fell asleep in her lap. Then the hunters cut off its horn.

It was said that only a gentle and pure maiden had the power to tame a Unicorn.

The Qilin from Chinese mythology is sometimes called the 'Chinese Unicorn' but it differs greatly in appearance (see right) and character. Despite its fearsome looks, it is considered to be a good omen, heralding peace or prosperity. It is so gentle that it can walk on grass without harming any insects, and it does not eat meat. Even so, it can become fierce and breathe fire if it sees a wicked person threaten a good person. In Japanese legend, it is called a Kirin and it looks more like a Western Unicorn than a Qilin but its body is covered in scales.

A Japanese woodprint showing a Baku.

Japanese mythology also has the Baku, another beneficial Chimera. It has been described as combining parts of the bodies of elephants, rhinos and tigers. The Baku appears in Japanese folk tales as a creature which devours people's nightmares.

Part-dragon, part-deer, and part-ox, the Chinese Qilin is also covered in scales.

The Bad...

Probably one of the scariest Chimeras is the Manticore, a creature with the body of a lion, and the head of a human, with three rows of savage, sharp teeth. It has the tail of a dragon or serpent which can shoot out poisonous spines or hairs to paralyse prey. It is said to range in size between that of a lion and a horse. The Manticore originated in Persian mythology, where its name meant 'man-eater'. It is thought to kill its victims instantly and to devour them, including their bones.

Tales of Manticores are still told in parts of Asia. If a person disappears, it is believed that the Manticore has eaten them.

The Ushi-oni is another terrifying Chimera which appears in Japanese folklore. There are various kinds of Ushi-oni, but all of them are monstrous and have the horned heads of cattle.

One kind of Ushi-oni is a huge, ferocious sea monster with the body of a crab and the head of a bull. It is said to live off the coast where it attacks fishermen.

The Tarasque was a fearsome monster that caused chaos and devastation across Provence, in France. Many knights tried and failed to capture it, until Saint Martha tamed it and led it back to the city where it was attacked and killed.

The Tarasque was a bizarre-looking Chimera with a lion's head, six bear-like legs, an ox-like body covered with a turtle's shell, and a scaly tail with a scorpion's sting.

Catoblepas

..And the Ugly

From Ethiopia comes a Chimera, called a Catoblepas. It is said to resemble a black buffalo, with a pig's head which is so large and heavy, it always hangs down to the ground. Like the Basilisk (see page 17), its stare and breath are reputed to be fatal, killing people or turning them to stone.

Centaurs carrying off nymphs.

22

Half-human, half-beast

The famous Centaur, Chiron, was a wise teacher of Greek heroes, including Achilles.

Strange-looking creatures composed of unexpected combinations of animals and humans have appeared throughout mythology since ancient times. They may be animals with human heads or torsos, or humans with animal heads.

An Onocentaur, with the top half of a human and the body of a donkey.

Centaurs

Half-horse, half-human, Centaurs first appeared in Ancient Greek mythology. They are said to be the sons or grandsons of Ixion, King of the Lapiths, and the goddess, Nephele. Centaurs may be as wild and untameable as horses, but they are also wise and brave teachers. They are often shown carrying off nymphs, when their wild side comes to the fore. Female Centaurs, called Kentaurides, appear in later Greek and Roman myths. The Onocentaur, half-human and half-donkey, appears even later.

Centaurs from Mesopotamia

Centaur-like creatures are also found in the ancient myths of Mesopotamia. The Urmahlullu, or 'lion-man', is a guardian spirit with the body of a lion and the head and torso of a human. Centaurs with lions' bodies also appear in English heraldry.

Some Mesopotamian Centaurs have the bodies of scorpions. In the famous Epic of Gilgamesh, they stand guard outside the gates to the land of the Sun god, Shamash. They open the gates as the Sun god rises.

In Mesopotamia, statues of the Urmahlullu stood outside the rooms where the priests ritually washed.

Scorpion men are called Aqrabuamelu or Girtablilu. It is said that they were created by the sea goddess, Tiamat, to wage war against the other gods.

23

Snake People

In Hindu mythology, Nagas are serpent gods that play an important part in religion. They are often half-human, half-snake, or snakes with multiple heads, each one hooded like a cobra's. Nagas protect wells and rivers, and control life-giving rainclouds. Hugely powerful, their only enemy is the giant bird-man, Garuda (see page 14). Tales about Nagas are also commonly found in Buddhist mythology. Chinese tales feature Nuwa, a creature that is half-woman, half-snake. She is said to have created humans out of lumps of clay, and to have repaired the sky after a terrible catastrophe destroyed the world.

Nuwa and her husband Fuxi

A female Naga is called a Nagini. Legend says that Nagas are dangerous to humans but only if they have been provoked or angered.

Pan is famous for his music. It can inspire people or cause panic, depending on his intentions.

Satyrs and Fauns

The Satyrs of Greek mythology are woodland creatures who are human down to the waist, apart from pointed ears and horns, but have the hairy legs and hooves of a goat. They are the pleasure-loving followers of Pan, the god of shepherds and hunting, who is often shown playing pipes. Their favourite occupations are drinking wine and chasing nymphs. Their counterparts in Roman myths are known as Fauns. A similar half-human creature from Greek legend is an Ipotane, meaning 'horse-person'.

An Ipotane has a horse's hindquarters, legs and tail, with the head and upper body of a human.

24

The Minotaur

The famous Minotaur of Greek mythology is a terrible monster with the body of a man and the head of a huge bull. His father is a white bull sent to King Minos of Crete by Poseidon, the sea god; his human mother, Pasiphae, is King Minos's wife. The Minotaur lives deep inside the maze-like Labyrinth, which Minos has built to contain him. After defeating Athens in war, Minos demands that the Athenian king send seven boys and seven girls every year to be devoured by the Minotaur. The Athenian hero, Theseus, finally succeeds in killing the Minotaur.

In Greek, Minotaur means 'Bull of Minos'. The historical site of Knossos in Crete is thought to be the site of the Labyrinth.

Animal-headed gods

Many cultures revere deities with animal heads. In the Hindu religion, Ganesha, the elephant-headed god, is one of the best-known and most honoured gods. He is believed to remove obstacles and is worshipped at the beginning of every new task. Most stories tell how Ganesha, the son of the goddess, Parvati, and the great god, Shiva, is born with a human head and body. When Shiva beheads him in a quarrel, she replaces Ganesha's head with that of an elephant.

In Ancient Egypt, many deities were portrayed with the heads of animals. Among them are Bastet, a goddess with the head of a cat, and Sobek, a god with the head of a crocodile.

An ancient name for Ganesha is 'Ekadanta' or 'One-tusked'. This refers to the fact that he has only one whole tusk, the other having broken off.

The Ancient Egyptian gods, Bastet and Sobek.

Dog-headed

A dog-headed human is called a Cynocephalus. Tales of dog-headed people can be traced back to ancient Greece. These creatures also feature in many writings from medieval times. They are often used to depict people from far-distant lands who appeared outlandish to early explorers.

An illustration of a Cynocephalus from a 15th-century printed book.

Man or Caiman

The legend of El Hombre Caiman, or the 'Caiman Man', comes from the north coast of Colombia in South America. He is said to have been a fisherman originally, who is enchanted by a river spirit and turned into a caiman. He returns to the river once a year to hunt for human victims to feed on.

El Hombre Caiman

Cow face

The Chichevache is a cow with a human face that appears in European mythology. It is said to prey on good wives but to be constantly starving due to women being unfaithful to their husbands. Whereas, it is said that the Bicorne, a type of two-horned Unicorn, is always fat and well fed because it only eats kind and obedient husbands, and they are in plentiful supply.

The Chichevache

Medusa

In Greek mythology, Medusa is one of three monstrous sisters, called the Gorgons. Originally a beautiful nymph, Medusa offends the goddess, Athene, who turns her flowing locks of hair into writhing snakes and makes one glance from Medusa turn a person into stone. Medusa is eventually killed by the hero, Perseus, who looks at her reflection in his shield to guide him, then cuts her head off. Two beings spring from her blood - Pegasus, the winged horse (see page 11), and the giant, Chrysaor.

Perseus gives Medusa's head to Athene, to place on her shield for protection.

Fig: 3.

Vir marinus episcopi spicie An 1531 captus m mari Baltico.

An engraving of a Merman, supposedly caught in the Baltic Sea in the 16th century.

A Mermaid has the head and upper body of a woman and the tail of a fish. Stories of Mermaids may have been based on sightings of sea animals, such as dolphins or manatees.

Mere Folk

Legends of magical creatures that are half-human and half-fish abound. Stories of Mermaids date back at least as far as Ancient Assyria. A goddess called Atargatis falls in love with a mortal shepherd and, by doing so, causes his death. Filled with remorse, she jumps into a lake and takes the form of a Mermaid.

Sighting a Mermaid was often unlucky and foretold disaster. Some Mermaids, much like Sirens (see page 12), would sing to sailors, thus enchanting them and causing shipwrecks. They were also said to drag drowning men down into their undersea kingdoms. In some stories, they can only become immortal by marrying a human being. The less common, male equivalent of the Mermaid is the Merman. The most famous may be the Greek god, Triton, son of the sea god, Poseidon.

Other fish-like people include the Rusalki of Russia, the Jengu of Cameroon and the Merrow of Ireland and Scotland. The Melusine of European folklore are believed to be spirits of sacred rivers and streams. Like Mermaids, they have the body of a woman but are sometimes shown with wings and two tails.

Other mythical water creatures include Selkies from Scotland who can transform themselves from seals into humans by removing their animal skins (see page 40).

The Ichthyocentaur, or fish centaur, was an extraordinary creature with a human body, a fish's tail and the front legs of a horse.

A Sea Monk is said to be a monstrous fish that looks like a monk.

27

A Kraken attacks sailors and their ship.

Water Beasts

Some of the largest creatures in mythology are water beasts, in particular those that live in the oceans. Reports from sailors, even today, tell of strange and fearsome monsters that attack them and their ships.

A boatful of unfortunate sailors land on the Aspidochelone's back.

Sea Serpents and other Monsters of the Deep

Sea serpents appear in many mythologies, especially those of maritime countries. Some people believe that they are actual sea creatures, such as whales or sharks, exaggerated in size and danger by frightened sailors. Others think that they might be the sole surviving examples of prehistoric sea reptiles. Sea serpents are usually reported as being gigantic creatures.

The Aspidochelone, known from medieval texts, is supposed to have been the size of an island. In Norse mythology, Jormungandr (see page 9) is so long, its body can encircle the whole world. A serpent, some 20 metres long, was sighted in 1848 by the crew of HMS Daedalus while on an Atlantic voyage.

The Leviathan is a Biblical sea monster whose name has come to mean any enormous, whale-like sea creature.

In his book, 'History of the Northern Peoples', 16th-century Swedish writer, Olaus Magnus, describes many sea monsters such as this serpent.

The Kraken

The legendary Kraken of Scandinavian mythology is another enormous sea monster, with immense tentacles. Sailors not only feared the monster itself but the powerful whirlpool it created when it suddenly descended into the sea. This could suck down even the biggest of ships. It may be that the story of the Kraken originated from sightings of giant squid which really do exist.

An artist's impression of the Biblical Leviathan.

Scylla and Charybdis

In Greek mythology, Scylla and Charybdis are terrifying monsters that guard the two sides of a narrow channel, making it impossible for sailors to navigate it safely. Scylla is a grotesque sea monster with six snapping heads and a ring of snarling dogs around her waist. Originally a sea nymph, Charybdis takes the form of a gigantic whirlpool that sucks ships down to their doom. According to Homer's Odyssey, Odysseus is one of the very few who successfully navigated the channel by sailing closer to Scylla and losing six of his men to the monster.

When Scylla kills Odysseus's men, he takes the oars and helps to row the ship to safety through the strait.

Sea-horses and Sea-lions

Hippocampus is the Greek word for the tiny and unusual fish, known as sea horses in English. In Greek mythology, however, it is a huge creature with the body of a horse and the tail of a fish or dolphin that pulls the chariot of Poseidon, god of the sea. Fish-tailed creatures also appear in Etruscan legend. They include Leokampoi (fish-tailed lions), Taurokampoi (fish-tailed bulls) and Pardalokampoi (fish-tailed leopards).

Leokampoi and Hippocampus

The Nuckelavee

The Nuckelavee

A terrible sea-monster, the Nuckelavee is found in Celtic mythology. This hideous creature has partially-finned legs, and a horse's body with a human torso and head growing out of its back. Its enormous mouth gapes open, and its single eye burns with a red flame. More gruesomely still, the beast has no skin on its body. The Nuckelavee is said to live mainly in the sea but cannot cross running water, such as rivers and streams. It occasionally rampages across the land, spreading plague and causing crops to die.

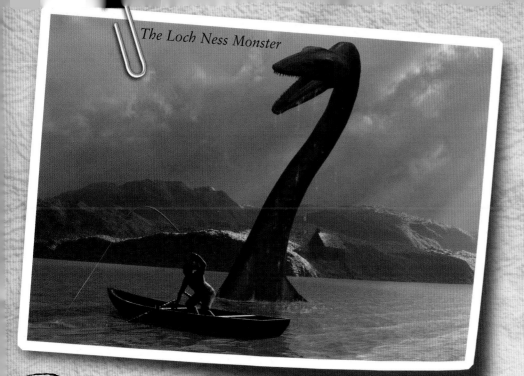

The Loch Ness Monster

Lake monsters

There have been numerous stories of huge animals living in lakes across the world. Although frequently sighted, no specimens have ever been caught and their existence has never been proven. Perhaps the most famous is the Loch Ness Monster, said to inhabit Loch Ness in Scotland. Similar monsters have been widely reported in North America, such as Ogopogo in Okanagan Lake, Champ in Lake Champlain, and Manipogo in Lake Manitoba.

Bunyips, Kappas and Kelpies

The Bunyip of aboriginal legend lies in wait for its prey in rivers, creeks, lakes and swamps. It is sometimes described as having a dog-like face, dark fur, a horse-like tail, flippers, and walrus-like tusks or horns.

Small children are one of the Kappa's favourite meals, although they will also eat adults.

Water spirits, called Kappas, are said to haunt rivers and ponds in Japan. They are believed to have scaly skin and webbed feet. In Scotland the Kelpie, or water horse, lures humans on to its back, then dives into the deepest lake and drowns its unfortunate victim.

A Bunyip creeping out of a swamp.

In Scandinavian mythology, Kelpies are known as brook horses.

Heracles and the Gigantes

Giants

Monsters of enormous size and strength appear in many of the world's myths and legends. The English word for these colossal beings is 'Giant', derived from one of the most famous ancient examples, the Gigantes, of Greek mythology.

The Gigantes

In Ancient Greece, the Gigantes are the giant children of the Gaia, goddess of the Earth, and Uranus, god of the sky. Furious that another group of her children, the Titans, has been imprisoned by the gods of Mount Olympus, Gaia encourages the Gigantes to wage war against the Olympians.

Led by Alcyoneus and Porphyrion, the Gigantes attempt to reach the top of Mount Olympus by stacking three other mountain ranges on top of each other.

Unperturbed, the Olympians call on the hero, Heracles (see page 37) for help. He kills Alcyoneus, then shoots Porphyrion with an arrow, after Zeus has struck him with lightning. The gods once more take control of the world and condemn the Gigantes to the underworld.

Atlas is the leader of the Titans who lost a war with the Olympian gods. Zeus condemns him to stand on the edge of the world and hold up the sky on his shoulders.

A painting by Marten Eskil Winge (1872) showing the final battle between the giants and the gods.

An ancient carving from India depicting the goddess Durga doing battle with the Daityas.

Other Warring Giants

In other mythologies, giants are frequently in conflict with the gods. Hindu giants, called Daityas, fight against the gods, with varying degrees of success. In Norse mythology, the Jotuns, or giants, often do battle with the gods, even though many are related to them by marriage. It is believed that at the final battle of Ragnarok, the Jotuns will storm Asgard and kill most of the gods. Another important Norse giant is Ymir, from whose body the world was created. Odin and his brothers used Ymir's flesh to create the earth. The blood of Ymir formed seas and lakes.

The Formorians

The war-like giants of Irish mythology are called the Formorians. It is thought that they represent the forces of chaos and nature. Legend tells how the Formorians fight off waves of settlers who come to live in Ireland but they are eventually defeated at the second Battle of Magh Tuireadh. The Formorians are led by the giant, Balor. In the battle, the hero, Lug, himself half-Formorian, kills Balor, then drives the defeated giants into the sea.

The giants of Irish mythology were called the Formorians.

Legend says that the Giant's Causeway on the coast of north-east Ireland was built by a giant.

Giant stones

Many legends tell how giants shape the landscape. The frost giants of Norse mythology are said to have carved out the rivers, valleys and fjords. They were born from the sweat of the giant, Ymir (see page 33), the first living being. The great god, Odin, killed Ymir and used his bones and teeth to make the rocks and mountains. The Giant's Causeway in Northern Ireland was built by the giant, Fionn mac Cumhaill (see page 36).

In Basque mythology, a race of giants called the Jentil, or Jentilak, live alongside humans. They are very tall and hairy and they can walk across the sea. They are so strong that they can hurl huge rocks down from the mountains which is said to explain the ancient stone monuments and standing stones found in the region.

A Jentil building an ancient monument.

34

One-eyed Giants

In Greek mythology, the Cyclops are enormously strong giants, with one eye in the middle of their foreheads. They make the weapons of the gods, and fight for the gods against the Titans. The Cyclops live as shepherds on an island of the same name.

Homer's Odyssey tells the story of the homeward journey of the hero, Odysseus, returning from the Trojan War. On his way, Odysseus and his men land on the island of Cyclops where the giant, Polyphemus, imprisons them in his cave and begins to eat them, one by one. To escape, Odysseus uses a stick to blind Polyphemus as he sleeps. When Polyphemus lets his sheep out of his cave, Odysseus and his men cling to the underside of the sheep to make their escape.

A Cyclops tends his flock of sheep.

A Troll rests in a forest.

Trolls

The Trolls of Scandinavian folk and fairytales are enormously strong and ugly creatures who leave their caves at night to hunt for human prey. Although dressed like human beings, they sometimes have a tail hidden inside their clothing. They have magical powers which they use to cause mischief and harm. Often invisible, they can also take the shape of animals and trees.

Ogres

Giants may be good or bad, but Ogres are always cruel and dangerous and are said to feed on human beings. They are first mentioned in 17th-century fairytales and have since appeared in many works of literature. Ogres are usually depicted with immensely strong bodies, large heads, and bushy beards.

In this painting by Italian artist, Giovanni Lanfanco, a couple are terrorised by a gigantic Ogre.

Rock hurler

The legendary Irish hero, Fionn mac Cumhail (Finn McCool) is also known as a giant. One of the many stories about his life and adventures tells how Fionn and his teacher, Finneces, catch the salmon of knowledge. Fionn accidently eats some of the salmon's skin, which means that he gains all the knowledge in the world. Legend has it that he built the Giant's Causeway (see page 34) as a roadway to Scotland. He is also said to have created the Isle of Man by tearing up part of Ireland and hurling it at a rival. It missed and landed in the sea. The empty space left behind became Lough Neagh.

Fionn mac Cumhail hurling part of Ireland which became the Isle of Man. Another smaller rock became the island of Rockall.

Talking Heads

In Welsh mythology, Bran the Blessed is a giant and a great king of Britain. His story is told in an ancient collection of tales, called the Mabinogion. Bran and his army fight the Irish over the mistreatment of Branwen, his sister. The Welsh win the war but only seven of their men survive. Bran, who is mortally wounded, orders his men to cut off his head and bury it in London. His head continues to talk to the men throughout the coming years.

Legend says that Bran's head is buried where the Tower of London stands today.

Hero Giants

In Homer's Iliad, the Greek hero and warrior, Ajax, is described as being immensely tall, strong and brave in battle. During the Trojan War, Ajax is chosen to fight the Trojan hero, Hector. Later, he quarrels with Odysseus over Achilles' armour and kills himself in shame.

Ajax is the most famous of the Greek warriors. He goes into battle, wielding a huge hammer and bearing a great shield made from seven ox-hides. When Achilles is killed, Ajax uses his hammer to fight off the Trojans so that he and Odysseus can get Achilles' body and take it safely back to their camp for burial.

Wrestling Matches

Antaeus, a giant of Greek myth, is the son of the gods, Gaia and Poseidon. Antaeus must remain in contact with the ground or he will lose his amazing strength. Antaeus challenges everyone he meets to a wrestling match. Ever the winner, Antaeus then kills his victims. But, legend says, the giant meets his match in Heracles. Discovering the secret of Antaeus's power, Heracles uses it to defeat the giant. Unable to throw him to the ground, Heracles lifts the giant into the air and crushes him in a bearhug.

Heracles crushing the giant, Antaeus, to death.

Biblical Giants

One of the best-known encounters between a giant and a human appears in the Bible. Goliath the giant Philistine warrior, challenges the Israelites to single combat. No one takes up the offer until David, a shepherd boy (and future King of Israel) steps forward.

Refusing any armour, David approaches Goliath, armed only with a sling and a few stones. He kills the giant with one stone, then cuts off his head.

Earth-shaking Giants

According to Maya legends, earthquakes are caused by the giant, Cabracan, tapping the mountains with his foot. The Hero Twins, Hunahpu and Xbalanque, set out on a quest to defeat the giant. Though gods, the Hero Twins fool the giant into thinking that they are simply mountain hunters. They trick him into eating a poisoned bird which robs him of his strength. His legs feel so weak that he cannot even lift his feet off the ground.

Hunahpu and Xbalanque meet the mountain-shaking giant, Cabracan.

A modern Werewolf transforming from human to wolf.

Shapeshifters

An 18th-century German woodcut of a Werewolf shapeshifting.

Almost every culture around the world has myths about shapeshifting. While the popular idea of a shapeshifter is of a human who magically transforms into an animal, there are numerous stories about animals that can also transform themselves.

Werewolves

Throughout northern Europe and North America there are legends of Werewolves. Arguably, the most famous of the shapeshifters, Werewolves are humans with the ability to transform themselves into ferocious, man-eating wolves, often at the time of a full moon. A person usually becomes a Werewolf because another Werewolf has bitten them or because they have been cursed. One way to kill a Werewolf is with a weapon made from silver, such as a bullet or a knife. A Werewolf always shifts back into human shape just before it dies.

Similar shapeshifters are found in many myths. Most of them involve humans transforming into other animals. In India, the Were-tiger is a sorcerer who terrorises livestock and might turn to eating people, instead, as its prey.

In Central and South America, the Were-jaguar is the most usual were-animal.

Perhaps the most famous Vampire, Count Dracula appeared in the 1897 novel by Bram Stoker.

Vampires

In legends, ancient and modern, Vampires are living corpses who pierce their victims' skin with their terrifying fangs and suck their blood. Vampires are active only at night. As daylight approaches, they must return to the safety of their coffins. They are said to be able to shapeshift between human and bat form.

A Navajo Yeenaaldlooshi is usually shown as naked, except for a coyote or wolf skin.

A Strigoi rises from its grave.

Souls of the dead

In Romanian mythology, Strigoi are evil souls of the dead that rise from their graves at night. They transform into animals or ghosts and haunt the countryside, terrorising anyone they happen to meet. They are said to be closely related to Werewolves (see page 39).

Selkies and Swan Maidens

Some shapeshifters can change their form only if they have an article of clothing or a layer of skin. The legendary Selkies of Scotland can transform themselves from seals into humans. To do this, they shed their seal skins, then put them back on to turn into animals again. Likewise, the Swan Maidens of Norse legend must wear a magical robe of swan feathers in order to shapeshift from humans into swans.

Swan Maidens bathing, having taken off their swan robes.

A Selkie reaches for her seal skin.

yo

Skinwalkers and Berserkers

Some Native American myths tell of shapeshifting Skinwalkers or humans who are able to transform themselves into any animal they wish. One of the best-known Skinwalkers is the Yeenaaldlooshii of Navajo legend. It is most commonly seen as a wolf, coyote, owl, crow or fox. Skinwalkers are greatly feared because they attack humans and can steal a person's skin, or soul, by staring into their eyes.

In Norse legend, assuming an animal's shape also means assuming its character. The famous Berserkers are warriors who wear bear skins, and fight with the strength and ferocity of a bear. Equally fierce are the warriors, called Ulfhednar, or 'wolf-coats', who wear wolf skins on their heads when they go into battle.

Egyptian gods, Horus and Seth

Many-tailed Foxes

Fox-like creatures appear often in Japanese mythology. Known as Kitsune they are said to be wise and intelligent. The more tails a Kitsune has, the wiser it is said to be. Kitsune also possess magical powers and can change shape and transform themselves into humans.

A 19th-century print, showing the Japanese Prince Hanzoku being tormented by a Kitsune.

Shapeshifting Gods

The Egyptian god, Seth, changes into a pig, then a hippo before being defeated by Horus. In Greek legend, Zeus shapeshifts to win the attention of mortal women. He appears to Europa as a white bull, to Leda as a swan, and to Danae as a shower of gold.

Europa is carried off by Zeus, disguised as a white bull.

A demon bursts from the depths of Hell.

Demons, Ghouls & Ghosts

Creatures that represent evil and darkness are an important concept in many religions, cultures and folklores. The opposite of goodness and purity, demons and ghouls bring terror to people, while witches are often considered malevolent.

Demons come in many forms, such as Buer, the demon leader, who is shown here with a lion's head and five goats' legs surrounding his body.

A ferocious-looking Rakshasa appears in a temple painting (above).

A statue of an Oni, brandishing a club (below).

Demons

Demons are a fundamental part of many religions and are often found in opposition to the gods, God, or forces of good. Hindu demons, evil beings called Rakshasas, are in constant battle against the gods. Christian demons are considered to be angels who have rebelled against God. They are the cause of evil and ignorance in the world. Their leader is commonly known as the Devil, or Satan. The Japanese Oni are gigantic demons with sharp claws, fangs and two horns growing out of their heads. They are often shown carrying a club and dressed in tiger skin. Their skin is usually red or blue in colour. Oni may originally have been evil spirits who caused disease and disaster. More recently, they have been given a more protective role and are believed to ward off bad luck.

In different cultures, the Devil has different names, including Abbadon, Angra Mainyu, Satan, Asmodai, Beelzebub, Lucifer, Belias and Iblis.

Gargoyles and Grotesques

Stone carved Gargoyles decorate cathedrals and churches, and have a spout to carry rain water away. A Grotesque is similar but does not function as a waterspout. Gargoyles are often monsters or demon-like creatures. They are believed to protect the building from evil spirits.

One of the many Gargoyles which look down from Notre Dame Cathedral in Paris, France.

Ghoul

In ancient Arabian legends, a ghoul, or gul, is a monstrous demon that can take the shape of an animal, especially a dog or hyena. It lives in the desert and lures travellers into its den where it kills and eats them. It also haunts graveyards where it opens graves and feasts on the dead. In European literature, ghouls live among the undead, alongside zombies (see below). Once human, these hideous creatures live off human flesh and cannot tolerate sunlight.

A ghoul raids a desert graveyard.

Zombies are popular in modern horror films.

Djinn

In the religion of Islam, Djinn are invisible beings created by Allah (God). They can choose to be good or evil. They live in places that are unclean, and cause fear and confusion when they meddle in human affairs. Sometimes, they attempt to take over human bodies. The chief of the Djinns is Shaitan, or Iblis. He disobeys Allah and becomes the enemy of humans, turning them away from Allah.

Djinns, or Genies, are also found in folk tales from Arabia, Persia and India. In the story of Aladdin, the Djinn, imprisoned in an old brass lamp, obeys whoever rubs the lamp and sets it free.

Zombies

Zombies are corpses that have been brought back to life. They originated on the island of Haiti where they play an important part in Voodoo beliefs. Revived by a sorcerer, they remain under his control because they have no free will of their own. In modern horror films, Zombies are usually shown as robotic, flesh-eating creatures whose bodies have begun to decompose.

A Djinn is made from fire and can take any form it chooses.

A painting of Baba Yaga

Hags, Witches and Banshees

Hags are generally depicted as wizened old women and appear in myths and folk tales from around the world. Though sometimes good and fairy-like, Hags are often considered malevolent, causing nightmares (see below), and frightening children. One famous and hideous Hag is Baba Yaga who appears in many Eastern European myths. She lives deep in the forest in a log cabin that stands on chicken's legs, surrounded by a fence of spikes, each with a human skull on top. Most stories tell how she kidnaps children, her favourite food, and brings about storms and tempests. However a few stories tell how Baba Yaga helps people who are lost.

In Irish mythology, a Banshee is a female spirit, or fairy, who is seen as a bringer of death. Her wailing voice can be heard if someone is about to die. Banshees are often described as wearing white or grey, with long, fair hair.

A Banshee may wail softly for a peaceful death; more loudly for a violent one.

The three witches from Shakespeare's Macbeth, illustrated by Arthur Rackham.

The stuff of Nightmares

A Mara, or Mare, is a female demon from Scandinavian mythology. Mares are said to move about at night, entering rooms through keyholes or under the door. They crouch on a sleeper's chest, causing bad dreams, hence the name - nightmares.

The Nightmare, painted by Henry Fuseli in 1781.

Glossary

Aboriginal
Referring to the Aborigines, the original inhabitants of Australia who arrived there thousands of years ago.

Arthurian
Stories relating to the time of King Arthur, a legendary British king.

Beneficial
Something good and positive.

Benevolent
Helpful, friendly or kindly.

Caiman
A reptile related to alligators and crocodiles.

Coyote
A dog-like animal that lives in the deserts and prairies of North America.

Deity
Another word for a god or a goddess.

Extinct
A plant or animal, real or mythical, that has died out and can never exist again.

Fjords
Long, narrow inlets of the sea which run between steep, high cliffs, commonly found in Norway.

Folklore
The traditional stories and legends of a people or culture that sum up their beliefs and often describe events that happened in their past.

Heraldic
Relating to heraldry. Heraldry is the symbolic images, decorations and colours used to represent a ruler, or an important person or family. Heraldic symbols were originally used on armour, flags and shields.

Hero
In Greek mythology, a hero was a being of amazing courage and strength who was often half-mortal, half-god.

Hoards
Large collections or stores of something, such as a dragon's treasure.

Icon
A Christian religious picture, painted on wood and displayed in some Christian churches.

Iliad
A great Ancient Greek poem, said to have been composed by Homer in the 8th or 9th centuries BC. The work is based on the legend of the Trojan War.

Immortality
Never dying but living for ever.

Invulnerable
Not able to be wounded or hurt.

Legends

Traditional stories which are often based on supposedly historical events. Like myths, legends were originally passed down by word of mouth by storytellers.

Malevolent

Wishing evil on others; another word for malicious.

Manatees

Large, air-breathing sea mammals, sometimes called sea cows. Sailors may have mistaken them for mermaids.

Maritime

Relating to the sea.

Medieval

Relating to the Middle Ages, a period of European history which lasted from around the 5th century to the 15th century AD.

Myths

Traditional stories, not based in historical fact but using supernatural characters to explain human behaviour and natural events. Myths helped ancient people to understand the world around them.

Nymph

In Greek mythology, a nymph was a spirit of nature who appeared as a beautiful girl.

Odyssey

A great Ancient Greek poem, said to have been composed by Homer, in the 8th or 9th centuries BC. It tells of the adventures of the hero, Odysseus, as he returned from the Trojan War.

Quest

In medieval legends, an expedition by a knight or group of knights to accomplish a task, such as the search for a mythical beast.

Quetzal

A bird from tropical Central America which has beautiful red and green plumage. Its feathers were highly prized by the Aztecs and other peoples of the region.

Sacrifices

When humans or animals are killed and offered to the gods or goddesses in order to win their favour.

Sorcerer

A person who uses magical powers. Another word for a witch or a wizard.

Supernatural

Magical beings, such as fairies, ghosts and gods, and events that cannot be explained by physical or scientific laws.

Torso

The trunk, or top part, of a human body.

Voodoo

A religion which is practised mainly on the Caribbean island of Haiti.

Index